ARSENAL

OFFICIAL ANNUAL 2024

Written by Josh James
Designed by Adam Wilsher

A Grange Publication

ISBN 978-1-915879-10-3

THE FA COMMUNITY SHIELD 2023

CELEBRATING ENGLAND FOOTBALL

CONTENTS

WELCOME

I want to start by saying a big thank you to all of our supporters.

Since I returned here as manager in 2019, I have witnessed the way the club has come together in all aspects. We have returned to that feeling that we all need in order to keep moving forward, that feeling of togetherness.

Something special is behind us all as a club – players, coaches, staff, supporters – every single one of us. And that is a feeling of unity and togetherness. It's the only way forward.

Without that it's impossible to build anything on the pitch or off it. So I want to thank all of our supporters for bringing the passion and energy that our players need every single day to reach our objectives.

Everyone at this club – from the men's first team, women's team, youth teams – we all want to give everything to achieve what this club deserves, and we will continue to do that. With passion, determination and pride. Everybody wants to deliver.

You cannot imagine how much it helps the players, how much belief it gives them, when they feel the energy from our supporters.

Wherever in the world you are and however you show your support, without you behind us, nothing we do makes any sense. You are our energy, you are living the game with us. You have always been in our attitude, in our self-belief. In the demands that push each other to seek excellence.

So that's what we all must do. Demand more from each other. Support each other. Be connected in every action, in every win, in every single ball.

In this book you can relive last season, get to know the players, and remember some special memories we have made along the journey so far. But we know we all want more, so we have to focus on what's in front of us, and if we keep moving forwards, we can achieve anything.

So thank you once again, for your unconditional love you have shown the players, and for being a part of us on our journey.

MIKEL ARTETA

ROLL OF HONOUR

League champions: 1931, 1933, 1934, 1935, 1938, 1948, 1953, 1971, 1989, 1991, 1998, 2002, 2004
FA Cup winners: 1930, 1936, 1950, 1971, 1979, 1993, 1998, 2002, 2003, 2005, 2014, 2015, 2017, 2020
League Cup winners: 1987, 1993 **European Fairs Cup winners:** 1970
European Cup Winners' Cup winners: 1994
Charity/Community Shield winners: 1930, 1931, 1933, 1934, 1938, 1948, 1953, 1991 (shared), 1998, 1999, 2002, 2004, 2014, 2015, 2017, 2020, 2023

2022/23
SEASON
REVIEW

AUGUST

We got the new Premier League season underway in fine style on a Friday night under the lights at Selhurst Park. With debutants William Saliba, Gabriel Jesus and Oleksandr Zinchenko all impressing, we ran out 2-0 winners to set the tone for a perfect opening month. Jesus got his first goals for us the following week in a comfortable home win over Leicester City, and we raised the level again for the trip to Bournemouth. Captain Martin Odegaard netted twice in the opening 11 minutes, and Saliba added a superb third, on the day his 'Saliba!' chant was born in the away end. Back at the Emirates, Odegaard scored again before Gabriel came up from defence to seal a late comeback win over Fulham. The Emirates was rocking once more on the last day of the month against Aston Villa, when Brazilian duo Jesus and Gabriel Martinelli both scored to make it five wins out of five at the start of the season. Mikel Arteta was named Premier League Manager of the Month and we sat proudly on top of the table heading into September.

ARSENAL.COM PLAYER OF THE MONTH **GABRIEL JESUS**

RESULTS

Fri 5	Premier League	**Crystal Palace** (A)	**2-0**	*Martinelli, Guehi (og)*
Sat 13	Premier League	**Leicester City** (H)	**4-2**	*Jesus 2, Xhaka, Martinelli*
Sat 20	Premier League	**Bournemouth** (A)	**3-0**	*Odegaard 2, Saliba*
Sat 27	Premier League	**Fulham** (H)	**2-1**	*Odegaard, Gabriel*
Wed 31	Premier League	**Aston Villa** (H)	**2-1**	*Jesus, Martinelli*

SEPTEMBER

At Old Trafford Gabriel Martinelli's opening goal for us was controversially ruled out following a VAR review for a foul in the build up, and the hosts inflicted our first defeat of the season, despite Bukayo Saka's equaliser on the hour mark. We returned to European action after a year's absence with a trip to Switzerland in the Europa League, and claimed a 2-1 victory thanks to Brazilian winger Marquinhos netting his first goal for the club, then setting up Eddie Nketiah for the winner. After a short break, we inflicted Brentford's heaviest ever home defeat in the Premier League. The goals came from Saliba, Jesus and summer signing Fabio Vieira – smashing home a beauty to open his Gunners account. The match was also significant for the introduction of academy product Ethan Nwaneri late on. His appearance made him the youngest player in the club's history – at the age of 15 years and 181 days – and indeed he also broke the all-time Premier League record for youngest player too.

RESULTS

Sun 4	Premier League	**Manchester United** (A)	1-3	*Saka*
Thu 8	Europa League	**FC Zurich** (A)	2-1	*Marquinhos, Nketiah*
Sun 18	Premier League	**Brentford** (A)	3-0	*Saliba, Jesus, Vieira*

OCTOBER

October began with a bang – a memorable 3-1 home win in the north London derby. Midfielder Thomas Partey got the ball rolling with a super 20-yard strike into the top corner before the visitors struck back with a Harry Kane penalty. But we were dominant after the break, adding further goals from Jesus and Granit Xhaka – who had started the season in excellent form. Liverpool were the next team dispatched at the Emirates. Martinelli scored inside the first minute, but it took a second-half penalty from Saka to win the game after Liverpool twice equalised. Saka was on target again in our nervy win at Leeds and we dropped points for only the second time this season in a 1-1 draw away to Southampton. We returned to the top of the table at the end of the month though after a thumping win over Nottingham Forest. Reiss Nelson scored a brace in our biggest victory of the season. In Europe we had home and away clashes with both Bodo/Glimt of Norway and Dutch side PSV Eindhoven, winning three of the four matches to assure qualification to the knock-out stages.

RESULTS

Sat 1	Premier League	**Tottenham Hotspur** (H)	3-1	*Partey, Jesus, Xhaka*
Thu 6	Europa League	**Bodo/Glimt** (H)	3-0	*Nketiah, Holding, Vieira*
Sun 9	Premier League	**Liverpool** (H)	3-2	*Martinelli, Saka 2*
Thu 13	Europa League	**Bodo/Glimt** (A)	1-0	*Saka*
Sun 16	Premier League	**Leeds United** (A)	1-0	*Saka*
Thu 20	Europa League	**PSV Eindhoven** (H)	1-0	*Xhaka*
Sun 23	Premier League	**Southampton** (A)	1-1	*Xhaka*
Thu 27	Premier League	**PSV Eindhoven** (A)	0-2	
Sun 30	Premier League	**Nottingham Forest** (H)	5-0	*Martinelli, Nelson 2, Partey, Odegaard*

ARSENAL.COM PLAYER OF THE MONTH **GRANIT XHAKA**

NOVEMBER

A narrow 1-0 win over FC Zurich at the Emirates – thanks to a first-half Kieran Tierney strike – was enough to secure top spot in our Europa League group, and receive a bye straight into the Round of 16. Back in domestic action we visited Stamford Bridge, securing a 1-0 win thanks to Gabriel's close-range finish from an inswinging corner just after the hour mark. At the Emirates we exited the Carabao Cup at the first hurdle, losing our third-round match against Brighton 3-1, despite Nketiah giving us a 20th-minute lead. We finished the first part of the season – before the World Cup break – with a tricky-looking trip to Wolves. Captain Odegaard put in another fantastic display, grabbing two more goals, to seal another victory as domestic football took a back seat for six weeks. We had dropped points from just two of our opening 14 Premier League games, going into the break five points ahead of second-placed Manchester City.

RESULTS

Thu 3	Europa League	**FC Zurich** (H)	1-0	*Tierney*
Sun 6	Premier League	**Chelsea** (A)	1-0	*Gabriel*
Wed 9	Carabao Cup	**Brighton & Hove Albion** (H)	1-3	*Nketiah*
Sat 12	Premier League	**Wolves** (A)	2-0	*Odegaard 2*

DECEMBER

After the World Cup in Qatar that had seen Saliba's France finish runners-up to Argentina, and Jesus picking up a knee injury while playing for Brazil, we were finally back on the pitch on Boxing Day. Apart from friendly matches against Lyon and AC Milan in Dubai and at home to Juventus, we hadn't played for 44 days, but we picked up where we left off, coming back from 1-0 down at half-time to beat West Ham 3-1 at home. Our win at the Amex on New Year's Eve was even more impressive. Saka put us ahead inside two minutes and goals from Odegaard and Nketiah made it 3-0 before Brighton threatened a comeback. Martinelli increased our advantage though and we signed off 2022 with our 14th league win of the season. The Premier League combined their monthly awards for November and December with Arteta winning his second Manager of the Month award of the season, and Odegaard taking the Player of the Month honour.

ARSENAL.COM
PLAYER OF
THE MONTH
BUKAYO SAKA

RESULTS

Mon 26	Premier League	**West Ham United** (H)	**3-1**	*Saka, Martinelli, Nketiah*
Sat 31	Premier League	**Brighton & Hove Albion** (A)	**4-2**	*Saka, Odegaard, Nketiah, Martinelli*

JANUARY

We were frustrated by a well-organised Newcastle side at the start of the month, ending our 100 per cent home record in the league with our only goalless draw all season. We responded in style, though, with statement wins away to Tottenham and at home to Manchester United. At the Tottenham Hotspur Stadium, Saka forced goalkeeper Hugo Lloris into an own goal before Odegaard arrowed home from 20 yards to give us a two-goal half-time lead. And that was enough to take the points from a superb team performance. It was much closer against United, but an opportunistic finish from Nketiah in the last minute clinched a 3-2 win, and had the Emirates bouncing. Our FA Cup campaign started and finished in January. Nketiah scored twice in our 3-0 win away to League One side Oxford United in the third round, but we were edged out in the next round, going down 1-0 to Manchester City despite a strong showing at the Etihad Stadium.

RESULTS

Tue 3	Premier League	**Newcastle United** (H)	0-0	
Mon 9	FA Cup	**Oxford United** (A)	3-0	*Elneny, Nketiah 2*
Sun 15	Premier League	**Tottenham Hotspur** (A)	2-0	*Lloris (og), Odegaard*
Sun 22	Premier League	**Manchester United** (H)	3-2	*Nketiah 2, Saka*
Fri 27	FA Cup	**Manchester City** (A)	0-1	

FEBRUARY

Three games without a win at the start of February checked our progress. Everton scrapped to a 1-0 win at Goodison in Sean Dyche's first game in charge, to inflict only our second league defeat of the season. Back at home new signing Leandro Trossard scored his first Gunners goal, but we were pegged back by a Brentford equaliser. We surrendered our place at the top of the table following our next game, a 3-1 home defeat to Manchester City. Saka got us level from the penalty spot in the first half, but Jack Grealish and Erling Haaland scored in the final 20 minutes to make it 3-1. We looked to be heading towards more dropped points away to Aston Villa, with the score locked at 2-2 going into injury-time. Then up stepped January signing Jorginho to rifle home a shot from 20 yards, that went in off the back of former Gunners keeper Emi Martinez. Martinelli added a breakaway fourth to cap a spirited win. Back in the Midlands the following week, Martinelli's goal right at the start of the second half gave us a 1-0 win over Leicester, in which we restricted the hosts to just one shot all afternoon.

ARSENAL.COM PLAYER OF THE MONTH OLEKSANDR ZINCHENKO

RESULTS

Sat 4	Premier League	**Everton** (A)	0-1	
Sat 11	Premier League	**Brentford** (H)	1-1	*Trossard*
Wed 15	Premier League	**Man City** (H)	1-3	*Saka*
Sat 18	Premier League	**Aston Villa** (A)	4-2	*Saka, Zinchenko, Martinez (og), Martinelli*
Sat 25	Premier League	**Leicester City** (A)	1-0	*Martinelli*

MARCH

Martinelli continued his excellent form at the start of March, scoring twice as we saw off Everton at home. Saka was also on target as both players moved into double figures for goals for the season. Next up was one of the most dramatic games of the season. Bournemouth – struggling in the relegation zone – scored after just nine seconds, then made it 2-0 with half an hour remaining. We rallied, pulling level through Ben White and Partey. Then deep into six minutes of injury-time, Nelson rifled home a left-foot rocket to spark wild scenes of celebration. Jesus returned from injury to play a part in our comprehensive 3-0 win away to Fulham, and we made it four Premier League wins out of four in March with a 4-1 dismantling of Crystal Palace at home. In a month where we scored 14 goals and took a maximum 12 points, Arteta won his fourth Premier League Manager of the Month award while Saka was named Premier League Player of the Month.

It was a different story in Europe, though. After a promising 2-2 draw in Portugal, Sporting took us to extra-time in the return leg in London, and then triumphed on penalties to end our hopes in the competition. We lost both Takehiro Tomiyasu and Saliba to injury in the match, in what was the first penalty shoot-out for a first-team fixture at Emirates Stadium.

ARSENAL.COM
PLAYER OF
THE MONTH | LEANDRO
TROSSARD

Saturday 8th A

RESULTS

Wed 1	Premier League	Everton (H)	4-0	*Saka, Martinelli 2, Odegaard*
Sat 4	Premier League	Bournemouth (H)	3-2	*Partey, White, Nelson*
Thu 9	Europa League	Sporting CP (A)	2-2	*Saliba, Morita (og)*
Sun 12	Premier League	Fulham (A)	3-0	*Gabriel, Martinelli, Odegaard*
Thu 16	Europa League	Sporting CP (H)	1-1*	*Xhaka (*Sporting win 5-3 on pens)*
Sun 19	Premier League	Crystal Palace (H)	4-1	*Martinelli, Saka 2, Xhaka*

APRIL

Jesus scored his first goals since November in our resounding home win over Leeds to start the month and restore our eight-point advantage at the top of the Premier League table, albeit having played a game more than our only challengers Manchester City. That advantage looked to be increasing as we led Liverpool 2-0 in the first half at Anfield. The hosts roared back though, and only some heroics from Aaron Ramsdale in goal preserved us a point at the end of a breathless encounter. Once again we let a 2-0 lead slip in the next match, away to West Ham. We were two goals to the good inside 10 minutes, but failed to build on our fast start. Saka sent his penalty wide at 2-1, and the Hammers made us pay with an equaliser through Jarrod Bowen on 54 minutes.

A third successive draw meant that the title race was no longer in our own hands. Southampton went 2-0 up in the opening quarter of an hour, then restored their two-goal cushion after Martinelli had pulled one back. Odegaard gave us hope on 88 minutes before Saka equalised as the game entered injury-time. Trossard hit the bar late on, but the winner eluded us. It put the pressure on ahead of the huge showdown with Manchester City at the end of the month. It wasn't to be our night at the Etihad. City took control early on, and despite Rob Holding's late consolation, the hosts earned a vital win, that cut our lead at the top to two points, with City also having two games in hand. With five games remaining though, we had guaranteed Champions League qualification next season.

RESULTS

Sat 1	Premier League	**Leeds United** (H)	**4-1**	*Jesus 2, White, Xhaka*
Sun 9	Premier League	**Liverpool** (A)	**2-2**	*Martinelli, Jesus*
Sun 16	Premier League	**West Ham United** (A)	**2-2**	*Jesus, Odegaard*
Fri 21	Premier League	**Southampton** (H)	**3-3**	*Martinelli, Odegaard, Saka*
Wed 26	Premier League	**Manchester City** (A)	**1-4**	*Holding*

MAY

We bounced back with fantastic wins over Chelsea at home, with Odegaard scoring twice more, then away to Newcastle – inflicting only their second home defeat of the season. That 2-0 win at St James' Park ensured we could finish no lower than second, but we were still relying on Manchester City to drop points if we wanted to finish top. That task got even harder following a home defeat to in-form Brighton, then a 1-0 reverse away to Nottingham Forest, who ensured Premier League safety with the win. That result handed Pep Guardiola's side the title, but we finished the campaign on a high at Emirates Stadium. Xhaka, on his farewell appearance, scored twice before Saka curled home a beauty. Jesus and Jakub Kiwior – with his first goal for the club – completed the big win. It meant we amassed our highest-ever tally of goals for a Premier League season – 88 – and equalled our record for most Premier League wins in a season with 26.

RESULTS

Date	Competition	Opponent	Score	Scorers
Tue 2	Premier League	**Chelsea** (H)	3-1	*Odegaard 2, Jesus*
Sun 7	Premier League	**Newcastle United** (A)	2-0	*Odegaard, Schar (og)*
Sun 14	Premier League	**Brighton & HA** (H)	0-3	
Sat 20	Premier League	**Nottingham Forest** (A)	0-1	
Sun 28	Premier League	**Wolverhampton Wanderers** (H)	5-0	*Xhaka 2, Saka, Jesus, Kiwior*

AARON RAMSDALE

1

Born: Stoke-on-Trent, May 14, 1998

Nationality: English

Joined: from Sheffield United on August 20, 2021

Previous clubs: Bournemouth, Chesterfield (loan), AFC Wimbledon (loan), Sheffield United

Debut: v West Bromwich Albion (a), Carabao Cup, August 25, 2021 (won 6-0)

A larger than life presence on and off the pitch, goalkeeper Aaron played every minute of our Premier League campaign last season. Now in his third year at the club, our talented keeper twice won the Premier League Save of the Month award, for his stunning stops from Bournemouth's Dango Ouattara in March and Liverpool's Mo Salah in April. He kept 15 clean sheets throughout the campaign, including one in the Europa League. An England international since making his debut in November 2021, Aaron previously won Player of the Season awards with Bournemouth and Sheffield United, and was named London Football Awards Goalkeeper of the Year for 2023.

DEFENDER

BEN WHITE

4

Born: Poole, October 8, 1997

Nationality: English

Joined: from Brighton & Hove Albion on July 30, 2021

Previous clubs: Brighton & Hove Albion, Newport County (loan), Peterborough United (loan), Leeds United (loan)

Debut: v Brentford (a), Premier League, August 13, 2021 (lost 2-0)

First goal: v Bournemouth (h), Premier League, March 4, 2023 (won 3-2)

Having previously played in central defence for most of his career, Ben operated at right back for almost the entirety of last season, and was a revelation in the position. Fast, excellent in possession and a wonderful passer, the England international was one of the best defenders in the Premier League, playing all 38 games. He grabbed his first Gunners goal in the dramatic win over Bournemouth and also contributed five assists. A big money signing from Brighton in 2021, he was named Player of the Season for the Seagulls in 2020/21, and won Leeds United's Young Player of the Year award in 2019/20 while on loan. Ben was part of England's 2022 World Cup squad in Qatar.

GOALS, GOALS, GOALS!

Mikel Arteta's side scored more than 100 goals last season. Let's test your memory!

1. Who scored our final goal of the season?
A) Gabriel Jesus
B) Granit Xhaka
C) Jakub Kiwior

2. Which of these players did NOT score an own goal for us?
A) Emi Martinez
B) Hugo Lloris
C) Kieran Trippier

3. How many goals did we score in our Europa League group stage games in total?
A) 8
B) 10
C) 12

4. At which end of Emirates Stadium did we score more goals?
A) North Bank
B) Clock End
C) Same at both ends

5. Against which team did Ben White score his first-ever Arsenal goal?
A) Leeds United
B) Nottingham Forest
C) Bournemouth

7. Look at this picture. What was the final score in this game?
A) 2-1
B) 3-2
C) 4-3

8. What was the official time in the game of Reiss Nelson's winner against Bournemouth in March?
A) 95:57
B) 96:57
C) 97:57

9. Who scored a penalty in our home win over Leeds?
A) Gabriel Martinelli
B) Bukayo Saka
C) Gabriel Jesus

10. How many Premier League matches did we fail to score in?
A) 2
B) 4
C) 6

11. Who scored two FA Cup goals for us last season?
A) Mohamed Elneny
B) Fabio Vieira
C) Eddie Nketiah

12. How did Gabriel Martinelli score most of his goals?
A) Header
B) Right foot
C) Left foot

6. Look at this picture. Who provided the assist for this goal against Brighton?
A) Martin Odegaard
B) Bukayo Saka
C) Oleksandr Zinchenko

Answers on page 61.

GABBY, GABI OR GÁBI?!

The answers to all of these questions are either Gabriel Jesus, Gabriel Martinelli or Gabriel Magalhaes!

1. Scored the most goals for us last season.
2. **Got the most Premier League assists for us last season.**
3. Wears the lowest squad number.
4. **Is the oldest out of the three.**
5. Has also played for a French club.
6. **Made his Arsenal debut first.**
7. Has made the most appearances for us.
8. **Has won the most Brazil caps.**
9. Scored on his Arsenal debut.
10. **Got the most Premier League yellow cards last season.**

Answers on page 61.

PREMIER LEAGUE AWARDS

There were plenty of highlights for us in the Premier League season, and our performances didn't go unnoticed! Here's a list of the PL awards we won...

August
Manager of the Month – Mikel Arteta
Our perfect start was rewarded with Mikel's third-ever Manager of the Month award, after his previous successes in September 2021 and March 2022. We won all five of our games in the opening month, against Crystal Palace, Leicester City, Bournemouth, Fulham and Aston Villa.

November/December
Manager of the Month – Mikel Arteta
We won all four games in November and December, so Mikel duly took the top manager award again. We won three away games – against Chelsea, Wolves and Brighton, while also seeing off West Ham at home, opening up a seven-point lead at the top of the table.

Player of the Month – Martin Odegaard
The November and December awards were combined, due to the World Cup break, and our skipper won the honour for best player. Martin scored three goals and added three assists during his four appearances.

January
Manager of the Month – Mikel Arteta
We were unbeaten during January, taking seven points from our three games – all against high-flying sides. We drew with Newcastle before beating Tottenham Hotspur and Manchester United to maintain our lead at the top of the table.

March
Player of the Month – Bukayo Saka
Our winger enjoyed an incredible month, scoring three goals and adding two assists in his four appearances to earn his first-ever monthly award. He became the 22nd different Arsenal player to win a Premier League Player of the Month award, more winners than any other club.

March
Save of the Month – Aaron Ramsdale
Our keeper was at his brilliant best to deny Dango Ouattara at a crucial stage of our home win over Bournemouth.

March
Manager of the Month – Mikel Arteta
The boss picked up his fourth monthly award this season, after overseeing a perfect month in which we won all four league games – against Everton, Bournemouth, Fulham and Crystal Palace, scoring 14 goals in the process.

ALL-TIME MOST MANAGER OF THE MONTH AWARDS

Manager	Awards
Alex Ferguson	27
Arsène Wenger	15
Pep Guardiola	11
David Moyes	10
Jurgen Klopp	9
Martin O'Neill	8
Harry Redknapp	8
Rafael Benitez	7
Mikel Arteta	6
Sam Allardyce	6
Bobby Robson	6
Carlo Ancelotti	5
Eddie Howe	5
Kevin Keegan	5
Claudio Ranieri	5

ALL-TIME PLAYER OF THE MONTH WINS

Club	Players
Arsenal	22
Manchester United	21
Liverpool	17
Tottenham Hotspur	14
Chelsea	13
Manchester City	9
Everton	9
Newcastle United	7
Aston Villa	7
Southampton	6
West Ham United	6

April
Save of the Month – Aaron Ramsdale
Aaron won this award again after a fantastic flying save to deny Mohamed Salah at Anfield.

Season Gamechanger of the Season – Reiss Nelson

Reiss Nelson's display in our dramatic home win over Bournemouth was named as the most impactful performance in the whole of the Premier League. While we were 2-1 down in the must-win game, Reiss was brought on in the 69th minute to help us turn the game around. Within a minute he crossed for Ben White to equalise, but the real magical moment came in the seventh minute of injury-time. A corner was only half cleared to the edge of the box, and the winger struck it home left-footed into the top corner to spark wild scenes inside the Emirates.

DEFENDER

OLEKSANDR ZINCHENKO

35

Born: Radomyshl, Ukraine, December 15, 1996

Nationality: Ukrainian

Joined: from Manchester City on July 22, 2022

Previous clubs: Ufa, Manchester City, PSV Eindhoven (loan)

Debut: v Crystal Palace (a), Premier League, August 5, 2022 (won 2-0)

First goal: v Aston Villa (a), Premier League, February 18, 2023 (won 4-2)

An experienced Ukraine international with a host of honours to his name, Alex enjoyed a spectacular first season at the club, redefining the left-back role in the process. Although often starting games on the left of the back four, the boyhood Arsenal supporter likes to dictate play from the middle of the pitch, drifting into central areas where he puts his superb technique and passing range to great effect. He was named Arsenal Player of the Month in both January and February 2023. Previously with Manchester City, where he won four league titles and four League Cups, the 2019 Ukrainian Footballer of the Year scored his first ever Premier League goal in our win over Aston Villa in February 2023.

WILLIAM SALIBA

2

DEFENDER

Born: Bondy, France, March 24, 2001

Nationality: French

Joined: from Saint-Etienne on July 25, 2019

Previous clubs: Saint-Etienne, Nice (loan), Marseille (loan)

Debut: v Crystal Palace (a), Premier League, August 5, 2022 (won 2-0)

First goal: v Bournemouth (a), Premier League, August 20, 2022 (won 3-0)

It was an incredible debut season for William, who announced himself as one of the foremost central defenders on the continent with a series of impressive displays. The powerful, physically imposing Frenchman had spent most of the previous three years out on loan back in Ligue 1, but after making his long-awaited debut on the opening day of the 2022/23 season, he didn't look back. He scored his first goal for the club in just his third appearance, and barely missed a game until injury ruled him out of the run-in in March. A full France international who was part of the World Cup squad in Qatar, the highly-rated defender was named Ligue 1 Young Player of the Year in 2021/22 after a fantastic loan spell with Marseille. He signed a new long-term contract with the Gunners at the start of this season.

INSPIRATIONS

We asked our players to reveal their career inspirations, here's what they told us...

REISS NELSON

"For me, right now, the person I look at and think 'he's doing so well' is Bukayo. That's because of how young he is and how he just takes everything in his stride. For me that's such a great thing to see. He's come through the academy, taken that route, and he's done it perfectly. I think people underestimate how young he is and what he's actually achieving. For me Bukayo is an inspiration because any young player should want to be like him."

EMILE SMITH ROWE

"That was always my dad. From a very young age he always did absolutely everything he could for me to be able to play football. He always took me to the park behind our house with my older brother, so yes definitely, he was a main inspiration for me, and still is. There is no shortage of inspirational people for me to listen to now, and obviously the gaffer is so important for me at this stage of my career too. I always listen to him and try to take in as much as I can. The impact he has on players is just ridiculous, the way he speaks to us is brilliant."

WILLIAM SALIBA

"I had an Arsenal shirt when I was about seven or eight years old. I loved watching Arsenal. I had Henry on the back of my shirt, he was the one I looked up to the most. I loved watching him. Arsène Wenger was the manager, so there were a lot of French connections with Arsenal. I remember watching the big Champions League games, against Barcelona in the final I remember, but the other games too."

JORGINHO

"My mum is my big inspiration. She did everything to ensure that I would become the best I could be. She always tried to do the best she could to educate me and my sister, teaching us to be really good people in the future and not just look out for yourself. She has a background in football too, she still plays. In fact she plays three times a week. She absolutely loves football and we always talk about it. She normally tells me off when she thinks of something that I didn't do very well. I don't get many compliments from her to be honest! She is a tough coach for me!"

GABRIEL MAGALHAES

"Since a young age, I've always enjoyed watching Neymar play. We don't play in the same position, but he's certainly my idol. I'm still a big fan of his today. My inspiration away from football is my father. He battled hard for me to be here today. He'd always wake up early to go to work. He always wanted to get me into football. He's my inspiration off the pitch. He's a person who's always tried to do good things for me."

EDDIE NKETIAH

"My main inspiration is my family, I'm very close to them still. For everything they have done for me, and everything they've given me, they inspire and motivate me every day to get better. They always support me. It's my mum, my dad, two sisters – I speak to them every day. Literally every day I'll speak to them and during the week I'll see them as well, they come to the games as well so we are really close."

LEANDRO TROSSARD

"My granddad really inspired me, especially when I was younger. He didn't play himself, but he helped me a lot throughout my career. He was always there for me, supporting me, coming to games and everything. In fact he was the one training me to use my left foot as well. He always used to say that if you want to be a top player, you need to develop both feet. He said you have to be two-footed and he helped me with that."

MARTIN ODEGAARD

"My father was obviously a big inspiration for me. He was a player himself and I trained a lot with him, so of course that's where my interest in football came from. I remember I went to watch some of his games when I was growing up. I think the first time I ever went to watch a game in a stadium was one of my dad's games. He was playing in the top division in Norway and I was quite young at the time, maybe five or six years old. But I remember going to those games to watch him."

MOHAMED ELNENY

"Throughout my career, at whatever level I've played, I've always been at a team that can fight for the trophies. I need that to inspire me and motivate me. Some smaller clubs are just happy to stay in the league, or are not fighting for trophies. I cannot do that, I mean really I can't do that, I need the motivation of playing for something, to win. I am inspired by winning. Even when I play games with my kids! I need that competition."

BEN WHITE

"Just coming into work every day for a club like Arsenal is enough to inspire me. You have to be honest to yourself, come into training every day and become a better version of yourself. Just focus on yourself, don't judge yourself by other people's standards, be yourself. I'm here for what I can bring to the team, and that's what I need to work on every day, and try to be consistent every day at work. I look forward to training every day."

OLEKSANDR ZINCHENKO

"Everyone had their idols, and mine was Ronaldinho. For me I'd say he's the greatest player ever. Of course there is no doubt how good Lionel Messi is, and everyone has their own tastes and their favourites, but for me the best was Ronaldinho. When I was a kid, my inspirations were top, top footballers, because I was dreaming of being a footballer. But today my family are my big inspiration now, that's for sure."

DEFENDER

GABRIEL MAGALHAES

6

Born: Sao Paulo, Brazil, December 19, 1997

Nationality: Brazilian

Joined: from Lille on September 1, 2020

Previous clubs: Avai, Lille B, Lille, Troyes (loan), Dinamo Zagreb (loan)

Debut: v Fulham (a), Premier League, September 12, 2020 (won 3-0)

First goal: v Fulham (a), Premier League, September 12, 2020 (won 3-0)

Tough-tackling imposing defender Gabriel started all 38 Premier League games last season, underlining his status as one of the best centre backs in the country. The powerful left-footed defender also has an eye for goal, and netted three more last season, to take his overall club tally into double figures, including a vital late winner against Fulham in August 2022. Signed from French Ligue 1 side Lille, he netted on his debut in 2020 – also against Fulham – and has now racked up more than a century of appearances for the club. Three times voted Arsenal Player of the Month during his debut season, 'Big Gabi' has been capped by Brazil at youth level.

FORWARD

LEANDRO TROSSARD

19

Born: Maasmechelen, Belgium, December 4, 1994

Nationality: Belgian

Joined: from Brighton & Hove Albion on January 20, 2023

Previous clubs:
Genk, Lommel United (loan), Westerlo (loan), OH Leuven (loan), Brighton & Hove Albion

Debut: v Manchester United (h), Premier League, January 22, 2023 (won 3-2)

First goal: v Brentford (h), Premier League, February 11, 2023 (drew 1-1)

Experienced Belgium international Leandro settled seamlessly into life at Arsenal after joining during the January 2023 transfer window from fellow Premier League outfit Brighton & Hove Albion. After scoring his first goal in the home draw with Brentford, he notched a hat-trick of assists in our 3-0 win away over Fulham. Named Arsenal.com Player of the Month for March, he went on to rack up 10 Premier League assists for us, from just 20 appearances, second only to Bukayo Saka. Versatile, skilful and strong with both feet, Leo is effective in either a wide attacking role, or through the middle. Before moving to London he spent three and a half seasons at Brighton, scoring 25 times from 116 league outings, having previously played all his football in the Belgian league. He featured for his country at the 2022 World Cup in Qatar, having also had tournament experience with Belgium at Euro 2020.

SEASON REVIEW

SEPTEMBER

We kicked off the Women's Super League season with back-to-back 4-0 home wins, over Brighton and Tottenham respectively. Beth Mead was in excellent form from the off, scoring three times in the two games, including a superb strike in the north London derby in front of 47,000 at Emirates Stadium. The Champions League campaign also got off to a fine start – Vivianne Miedema, the matchwinner, back in the Netherlands to ensure a 3-2 aggregate win in the qualifying round.

RESULTS

Fri 16	Women's Super League	**Brighton** (H)	**4-0**	*Little, Blackstenius, Mead 2*
Tue 20	Champions League	**Ajax** (H)	**2-2**	*Blackstenius, Little*
Sat 24	Women's Super League	**Tottenham** (H)	**4-0**	*Mead, Miedema 2, Rafaelle*
Wed 28	Champions League	**Ajax** (A)	**1-0**	*Miedema*

OCTOBER

Jonas Eidevall's side racked up five straight wins in October, but the most notable was certainly the 5-1 thumping of European champions Lyon in France to kick off our Champions League group stage. Mead grabbed two more, as did Caitlin Foord, to inflict Lyon's heaviest ever defeat in the competition. We also became the first side for 17 years to score five against them in a single game. Closer to home, wins over Reading, Liverpool and West Ham extended the 100 per cent start in the league.

RESULTS

Sun 16	Women's Super League	**Reading** (A)	**1-0**	*Blackstenius*
Wed 19	Champions League	**Lyon** (A)	**5-1**	*Foord 2, Maanum, Mead 2*
Sun 23	Women's Super League	**Liverpool** (A)	**2-0**	*Walti, Maanum*
Thur 27	Champions League	**FC Zurich** (H)	**3-1**	*Nobbs, Hurtig 2*
Sun 30	Women's Super League	**West Ham United** (H)	**3-1**	*Nobbs, Blackstenius, Maanum*

VEMBER

r a comfortable 4-0 win at Leicester,
uffered our first defeat of the season –
g down to an injury-time winner against
chester United at Emirates Stadium. There
further bad news that afternoon, as Mead
ed her ACL and was later ruled out for the
son. We continued our good form in Europe
gh, Miedema's equaliser earning a draw
y to Juventus – managed by ex-Arsenal
s Joe Montemurro.

ARSENAL.COM PLAYER OF THE MONTH LAURA WIENROITHER

ESULTS

Sun 6	Women's Super League	**Leicester City** (A)	**4-0**	*Maanum, Foord, Catley, Blackstenius*
Sat 19	Women's Super League	**Manchester United** (H)	**2-3**	*Maanum, Wienroither*
Thur 24	Champions League	**Juventus** (A)	**1-1**	*Miedema*

ARSENAL.COM PLAYER OF THE MONTH VIVIANNE MIEDEMA

DECEMBER

Miedema continued her fine form at
the start of the month, scoring the only
goal in consecutive 1-0 home wins
over Everton and Juventus. Our prolific
striker netted again in the win at Aston
Villa, but was taken off at half-time of
our Champions League defeat against
Lyon, and, like Mead, would miss the
rest of the season with an ACL injury.
We finished the month with a huge 9-1
away win over FC Zurich to secure top
spot in our Champions League group.

RESULTS

Sat 3	Women's Super League	**Everton** (H)	**1-0**	*Miedema*
Wed 7	Champions League	**Juventus** (H)	**1-0**	*Miedema*
Sun 11	Women's Super League	**Aston Villa** (A)	**4-1**	*Corsie (og), Miedema, McCabe, Nobbs*
Thur 15	Champions League	**Lyon** (H)	**0-1**	
Wed 21	Champions League	**FC Zurich** (A)	**9-1**	*Maanum 3, Foord 2, Blackstenius 2, Little, Iwabuchi*

JANUARY

We were two minutes away from securing
a valuable home win over Chelsea
thanks to Kim Little's penalty, but Sam
Kerr grabbed a late equaliser for the
visitors. We completed the month with
comfortable wins in the two domestic
cup competitions – teenager Michelle
Agyemang scored her first senior goal for
the club in the 9-0 FA Cup win over Leeds.

ARSENAL.COM PLAYER OF THE MONTH FRIDA MAANUM

RESULTS

Sun 15	Women's Super League	**Chelsea** (H)	**1-1**	*Little*
Thur 26	Continental Cup	**Aston Villa** (H)	**3-0**	*Maanum 2, Foord*
Sun 29	FA Women's Cup	**Leeds** (H)	**9-0**	*Foord, Kuhl, Little, Hurtig, Beattie, Blackstenius 2, Agyemang, Pelova*

FEBRUARY

The highlight of the month was a superb extra-time win away to Manchester City to seal a place in the Continental Cup final – striker Stina Blackstenius with the all-important goal. However in the league we dropped precious points away to West Ham, and then away to Man City, and then exited the FA Cup in the fifth-round stage with a 2-0 defeat at Chelsea.

RESULTS

Sun 5	Women's Super League	**West Ham United** (A)	**0-0**	
Wed 8	Continental Cup	**Manchester City** (H)	**1-0**	*Blackstenius*
Sat 11	Women's Super League	**Manchester City** (A)	**1-2**	*Rafaelle*
Sun 26	FA Women's Cup	**Chelsea** (A)	**0-2**	

THE FA WOMEN'S CONTINENTAL TYRES LEAGUE CUP

WINNERS 2023

The FA Women's
Continental
League Cup

MARCH

We won the Continental Cup for the sixth time with a superb 3-1 comeback win over Chelsea at Selhurst Park. Despite falling behind on just two minutes, we roared back to lead 3-1 by half-time, and comfortably played out the second half to earn a deserved victory, and lift our first piece of silverware for four years. We followed it up with comfortable league wins over Liverpool and Reading before Champions League football resumed against Bayern Munich. We lost the first leg of the quarter-final 1-0 in Germany, but fought back at the Emirates in the return leg to progress 2-1 on aggregate. In between those two matches we beat Tottenham 5-1 to move back into the top three.

Sun 5	Continental Cup	**Chelsea** (N)	**3-1**	*Blackstenius, Little, Charles (og)*
Wed 8	Women's Super League	**Liverpool** (H)	**2-0**	*Blackstenius, Foord*
Sun 12	Women's Super League	**Reading** (H)	**4-0**	*Little, Maanum, Mukandi (og), Williamson*
Tue 21	Champions League	**Bayern Munich** (A)	**0-1**	
Sat 25	Women's Super League	**Tottenham** (A)	**5-1**	*Blackstenius, Foord 2, Little, Maanum*
Wed 29	Champions League	**Bayern Munich** (H)	**2-0**	*Maanum, Blackstenius*

RESULTS

APRIL

An absolute cracker from Katie McCabe gave us a 2-1 win over title-chasing Manchester City, but a 1-0 defeat away to Manchester United checked our progress. Also in that defeat to United, Leah Williamson was taken off with a knee problem, which proved to be a season-ending ACL injury. Attention then switched back to European football, and we came back from 2-0 down to earn a 2-2 draw away to Wolfsburg in the Champions League semi-final first leg.

ARSENAL.COM PLAYER OF THE MONTH LOTTE WUBBEN-MOY

RESULTS

Sun 2	Women's Super League	**Manchester City** (H)	2-1	*Maanum, McCabe*
Wed 19	Women's Super League	**Manchester United** (A)	0-1	
Sun 23	Champions League	**Wolfsburg** (A)	2-2	*Rafaelle, Blackstenius*

60,063

MAY

A club record crowd of 60,063 were there to cheer on the Gunners in the second leg of the semi-final, but it ended in heartbreak as Wolfsburg scored the winner in the last minute of extra-time. Also in that game full back Laura Wienroither became our fourth player of the season to suffer an ACL injury. The focus was then on securing a top three place in the WSL, and qualifying for Europe again next season. Straight wins over Leicester, Brighton and Everton followed, but a 2-0 defeat at Chelsea ended any remaining title hopes. Despite another 2-0 defeat at home to Aston Villa on the final day, we clinched a Champions League spot by finishing in the top three, edging out Manchester City on goal difference. Frida Maanum won the Arsenal Player of the Season award, after contributing 16 goals and nine assists from midfield.

ARSENAL.COM PLAYER OF THE SEASON KATIE McCABE

RESULTS

Mon 1	Champions League	**Wolfsburg** (H)	2-3	*Blackstenius, Beattie*
Fri 5	Women's Super League	**Leicester City** (H)	1-0	*Maanum*
Wed 10	Women's Super League	**Brighton & Hove Albion** (A)	4-0	*Blackstenius 2, Maanum, Pelova*
Wed 17	Women's Super League	**Everton** (A)	4-1	*Foord 2, McCabe, Wubben-Moy*
Sun 21	Women's Super League	**Chelsea** (A)	0-2	
Sat 27	Women's Super League	**Aston Villa** (H)	0-2	

WHO AM I?

Can you match the set of snappy clues to the player?

1. Pace No. 14 Record scorer	2. Captain England Defender

PATRICK VIEIRA

ROBERT PIRES

3. France Invincible Midfielder	4. Young Hale End Right wing

BUKAYO SAKA

TONY ADAMS

5. Magic feet Midfielder Spain	6. Brazil Young No. 11

MARTIN ODEGAARD

LEANDRO TROSSARD

7. France Defender Loans	8. Captain Norway Real Madrid

GABRIEL MARTINELLI

WILLIAM SALIBA

9. Goalkeeper Safe Hands Legend	10. Brazil Striker Man City

SANTI CAZORLA

THIERRY HENRY

11. Right back Centre back No. 4	12. France No. 7 Invincible

IAN WRIGHT

DAVID SEAMAN

13. Legend Striker Goals	14. Assists Belgium January signing

GABRIEL JESUS

BEN WHITE

Answers on page 61.

SPOT THE DIFFERENCE

Can you spot the six differences between these two images of Bukayo Saka and Declan Rice with the FA Community Shield? **Answers on page 61.**

MIDFIELDER

MARTIN ODEGAARD

8

Born: Drammen, Norway, December 17, 1998

Nationality: Norwegian

Joined (permanently): from Real Madrid on August 20, 2021

Previous clubs: Stromsgodset, Real Madrid, Heerenveen (loan), Vitesse (loan), Real Sociedad (loan)

Debut: v Manchester United (h), Premier League, January 30, 2021 (drew 0-0)

First goal: v Olympiacos (a), Europa League, March 11, 2021 (won 3-1)

Our Player of the Season for 2022/23, Captain Odegaard enjoyed an incredible year, scoring 15 goals and adding seven assists. One of the most creative and technically blessed players in world football, the attacking midfielder led by example, and passed the 100-appearance mark for the club towards the end of the campaign. Now in his fourth season at the club, having originally joined on loan in January 2021, Martin was a child prodigy growing up, signing for Real Madrid at the age of 16 and soon becoming their youngest-ever player. Now captain of the Norway national team as well, he made his senior national team debut at the age of 15 and 253 days in August 2014, becoming the youngest player in his country's history. He was nominated for the Premier League Player of the Season, Premier League Young Player of the Season and the FWA Footballer of the Year last term.

FORWARD

GABRIEL MARTINELLI

11

Born: Guarulhos, Brazil, June 18, 2001

Nationality: Brazilian

Joined: from Ituano on July 2, 2019

Previous club: Ituano

Debut: v Newcastle United (a), Premier League, August 11, 2019 (won 1-0)

First goal: v Nottingham Forest (h), Carabao Cup, September 24, 2019 (won 5-0)

It was another incredible year for tricky Brazilian forward Gabi, who jointly led our scoring charts with 15 goals last season, all in the Premier League. Usually operating on the left of the front three, the effervescent winger missed only three games in all competitions, and continued to impress with his direct running and fighting spirit. He equalled the Premier League record for most goals in a season by a Brazilian and signed a new long-term contract with us in February 2023. Previously with the youth setup at Corinthians, he joined Arsenal from third tier side Ituano shortly after his 18th birthday. He represented Brazil at the 2022 World Cup in Qatar, having won an Olympic Gold medal for his country at the 2020 Games in Tokyo.

39

WELCOME TO THE ARSENAL!

Jonas Eidevall made several additions to his playing squad last summer, including signing England ace Alessia Russo. Here's a bit more info on our new additions…

ALESSIA RUSSO

23

FORWARD

Born: Maidstone, February 8, 1999

Previous clubs:
Chelsea, North Carolina Tar Heels, Brighton, Manchester United

One of the stars of England's victorious Euro 2022 squad, Alessia joined us following the expiration of her contract at Manchester United, where she netted 26 goals from 59 appearances over three years.

Skilful and fast, Alessia started her career at Chelsea before moving to America, where she played alongside Lotte Wubben-Moy at North Carolina Tar Heels. She made her England debut in 2020, and scored four times at the 2022 European Championships, including an incredible backheel to nutmeg Swedish keeper Hedvig Lindahl in the semi-final. It was later named Goal of the Tournament, and she was ever-present as England lifted the trophy.

Shortly after joining Arsenal she was back in action for her country, helping the Lionesses reach the World Cup final in Australia and New Zealand, scoring three goals in the tournament.

After joining the Gunners, Alessia said: "It's time for a new challenge. You can see the project from last season and the history that the club's got.

"I'm really excited to get going, get into Champions League and into the league next season. The fight from the team and everything that they had thrown at them last season, I think they did amazing. I can't wait to be a part of it.

"I think the growth of the women's game has been extraordinary but particularly at a club like Arsenal. The sell-out against Wolfsburg was incredible and the fan base is something that's a huge part of this club and something that I'm really, really excited to be a part of as well."

CLOE LACASSE

24

Born: Ontario, Canada, July 7, 1993

Previous clubs:
Toronto Lady Lynx, IBV, Benfica

Experienced striker Cloe joined us from Portuguese champions Benfica, where she grabbed 100 goals from 129 appearances, 33 of them during a hugely successful season last term. She lifted eight trophies while with Benfica, including three league titles.

She made her senior debut for the Canada national team in 2021, and scored her first international goal against Argentina in October 2022. Prior to joining Benfica she represented IBV in Iceland, scoring more than 70 goals at better than a goal every other game.

Upon joining Arsenal, Cloe said: "I think with how my career has been going, it's just been an upward climb, especially over the last couple of years. I feel ready mentally and physically to be able to contribute here and win titles."

AMANDA ILESTEDT

28

Born: Solvesborg, Sweden, January 17, 1993

Previous clubs:
Karlskrona, Rosengard, Turbine Potsdam, Bayern Munich, Paris SG

Previously with some of Europe's biggest clubs, Amanda is an experienced and reliable central defender. She became our first signing of the summer when she arrived from PSG, where she won the Coupe de France in 2022. Before that she spent four years in Germany, and prior to that she won seven trophies in nine years with FC Rosengard in her homeland, working with Jonas Eidevall.

Amanda was a major part of Sweden's World Cup squad last summer, scoring three goals and eventually helping them finish in third place.

Speaking after signing, Amanda said: "I really want to win titles. It's a place that has really good facilities, and everything around the club and the team seems to be really good. Jonas definitely played a part in my decision to move. For me, he's one of the best coaches I've had."

LAIA CODINA

27

Born: Campllong, Spain, January 22, 2000

Previous clubs:
Barcelona, AC Milan (loan)

Part of Spain's free-flowing World Cup winning side, midfielder Laia Codina joined the Gunners from Barcelona in the summer.

The centre-back has already amassed a host of honours in her short career to date – winning three Spanish league titles, two Champions Leagues, one Spanish Cup and one Spanish Super Cup while with Barcelona – a club she joined at the age of 14. Laia then added the 2023 World Cup to that list, starting all four games after the group stages – including the final against England.

After completing the signing, head coach Jonas Eidevall said: "Laia is a world-class defender and I'm delighted to be working with her here at Arsenal. She has a great mix of technical ability and physical presence."

FORWARD

BUKAYO SAKA

7

Born: Ealing, London, September 5, 2001

Nationality: English

Joined: the academy on May 5, 2010

Previous clubs: None

Debut: v Vorskla Poltava (a), Europa League, November 29, 2018 (won 3-0)

First goal: v Eintracht Frankfurt (a), Europa League, September 19, 2019 (won 3-0)

Academy product Bukayo cemented his status as one of the most valuable talents in world football with another hugely impressive and consistent season. The dazzling winger, operating mainly on the right flank, didn't miss a single Premier League game for the second year in a row, and netted 15 goals in all competitions, as well as 11 assists. He was named Premier League Player of the Month in March, and finished as runner-up in the Arsenal Player of the Year award, having won the honour in each of the previous two years. An Arsenal player from the age of eight when he joined our Hale End Academy, he has been a full England international since 2020 and scored three times at the 2022 World Cup in Qatar. He signed a new long-term contract with the Gunners in the summer of 2023.

FORWARD

GABRIEL JESUS

9

Born: Sao Paulo, Brazil,
April 3, 1997

Nationality: Brazilian

Joined: from Manchester City on
July 4, 2022

Previous clubs:
Palmeiras, Manchester City

Debut: v Crystal Palace (a),
Premier League, August 5, 2022
(won 2-0)

First goal: v Leicester City (h),
Premier League, August 13, 2022
(won 4-2)

Explosive striker Gabriel enjoyed a hugely impressive first season at the club, contributing a combined 18 goals plus assists, despite missing a big chunk of the campaign through injury. Arriving from Manchester City in the summer of 2022, the Brazil international forward immediately became the focal point of the team's attack, and scored on his home debut against Leicester City. He was voted Arsenal.com Player of the Month for August, and continued to shine until picking up an injury while on duty with Brazil at the World Cup in Qatar. It was the second World Cup he'd featured in, having made his international debut as a teenager in 2016. An Olympic Gold medalist (2016) and Copa America winner (2019), he also won four Premier League titles while with City.

YOUNG

Jack Wilshere's under-18 team made it all the way to the FA Youth Cup final last season, a tournament we last won when Jack himself was a young player with us in 2009. Here are three of the standout performers from that cup campaign last term…

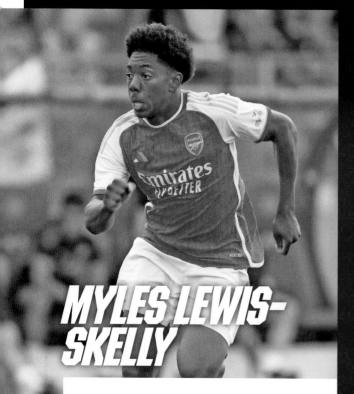

MYLES LEWIS-SKELLY

MIDFIELDER

Born: London, September 29, 2006
Joined Arsenal: May 16, 2015

A hugely gifted, powerful, driving central midfielder, Myles was one of the stars of our FA Youth Cup side last season. He played in six matches in the run to the final against West Ham, and scored the all-important extra-time winner against Manchester City in the semi-final at Emirates Stadium. A regular trainer with the first-team squad, he was part of the midseason training camp in Dubai during 2022/23 and also played seven times for our under-21 side while still a schoolboy. A member of our academy from the age of eight, he has developed rapidly season on season, and is also an England youth international. He played at the Under-17 European Championships in 2023, helping England reach the quarter-final.

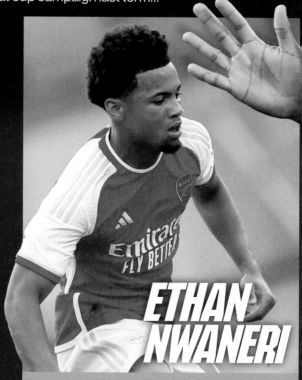

ETHAN NWANERI

MIDFIELDER

Born: London, March 21, 2007
Joined Arsenal: July 2016

In September 2022 Ethan became the youngest-ever first-team player in our history – smashing the previous record that had stood for nearly 20 years. The exciting attacking midfielder came on as a late substitute in our Premier League win over Brentford, at the age of just 15 years and 181 days. He broke the record of Cesc Fabregas, who was 16 years and 177 days old when he made his Gunners debut in 2003. In the process Ethan also broke the all-time Premier League record for youngest player for any club, and is the youngest to play in any top-flight match in English football. At home in the No. 10 role, Ethan joined our Hale End Academy aged eight in 2016, and has represented England at under-16 and under-17 levels. He scored twice in our run to the FA Youth Cup final last season.

GUNS

AMARIO COZIER-DUBERRY

FORWARD
Born: London, May 29, 2005
Joined Arsenal: October 7, 2019

The top scorer in our FA Youth Cup campaign last season with five goals from six appearances, Amario is an exciting, skilful attacker who usually plays on the right wing. As well as possessing a keen eye for goal, the London-born youngster loves to run at defenders and create chances for others. He was virtually ever-present for our under-21s last season, and also played for the first-team in the midseason friendly against Juventus at Emirates Stadium. An England youth international who joined the club as a 14-year-old, Amario regularly trains with the first-team squad, and was named on the bench several times for Mikel Arteta's side last term. He signed his first pro contract with us in June 2022.

Hi Joel! So first of all, why are you an Arsenal supporter?

I've been a fan since I can remember. Back at primary school I was absolutely Arsenal obsessed, had all the kit and things like that. My whole bedroom was covered in Arsenal stuff, the wallpaper, bed covers and I had a Gunnersaurus too. The full works, in fact I used to get this Annual every year as well – everything. I was full on and obsessed from a young age. But where it came from I don't know! I was just drawn to them. My dad's a Chelsea fan and my brother is a Man United fan so it definitely wasn't from my family!

What are your early memories of supporting the team?

My main memories were of watching Ian Wright, who was my hero. The number eight has always been my lucky number since I was young because of Ian Wright. Then came Marc Overmars, Nicolas Anelka, Emmanuel Petit, then the Invincibles, players like Dennis Bergkamp, Robert Pires – that was my childhood, watching those guys. But an early memory that really stands out for me is when Tony Adams scored at Highbury to win the league back in 1998. I was actually at

JOEL CORRY

Joel Corry is a Brit Award nominated, chart-topping DJ, but he's also a massive Gooner! We caught up with the football-mad music producer to ask him about his love for the Gunners, and what it was like to play in the same team as Jack Wilshere at Soccer Aid...

Hollywood Bowl that day, but I had to just stop bowling and watch that moment. I remember going crazy celebrating that goal, it was such an epic moment, especially as it was our captain who scored it. That's such a clear memory for me, a great moment.

Who is your all-time Arsenal hero?
It has to be Ian Wright. I just loved watching him, scoring goals week after week. The way he carried himself on the pitch, I loved it. Actually I was nominated for a Brit Award a couple of years ago and he was sitting at the table next to me. It was the first time I had met him in person, and I was starstruck. I was just trying to find the time to say hello to him, but before I could, he tapped me on the shoulder and said, "My kids love your music, can I get a selfie for them?" It was just a surreal moment for me! He was definitely a hero for me growing up, but there have been so many great players – Overmars, Thierry Henry of course, Anelka, Bergkamp – so many.

Do you have a favourite Arsenal goal?
Remember Ray Parlour's absolute screamer against Chelsea in the FA Cup final? That has to be up there, I love that one. I remember watching that game and when it went in it was a huge moment, I'd put that up there as my favourite goal.

What about a favourite kit?
Yes, the old yellow bruised banana kit with JVC on. They brought that back but I remember having that when it came out when I was younger, that was the best. I also had an old David Seaman purple top that I loved. I wasn't a goalie, but I had every kit and that was one of my favourites.

What do you think of the current team?
I think we're in a great place. We've got a young hungry squad and it feels like it's all gelling together properly. I'm buzzing to see what we can do. Last season was a big step forward, we have to look at it as a positive. We've signed our young players to new contracts, and strengthened the squad, so we are in a good position to move forward.

Do you manage to get to Emirates Stadium much?
I would love to go more, but literally every weekend I'm usually DJing, so it's really hard to get there with my schedule. I watch all the games on TV though. I'm on the road a lot DJing, and I have a tour manager I travel with, so I can't be with my mates watching in the pub unfortunately! Usually I'm in a random country somewhere, trying to find coverage of the game at whatever time the game kicks off in whatever timezone I'm in! A lot of my mates growing up were Arsenal fans too, so we would watch the games together when I was younger. I've been a few times to the Emirates, and it's always a great experience, but the way my life is now, I'm never really in the country to be honest. With Champions League nights back though that might make it easier for me. I would love to go to an away game in Europe!

Do you play much as well?
I used to play a lot when I was younger, I'm 34 now – getting old! But yeah I played all the time in school, lunchtime, after school, then at weekends for my Sunday League team. In my 20s I got more into the gym and fitness, so didn't play as much, but last summer I got the call

up to play at Soccer Aid and I didn't hesitate at all, I said yes immediately, and I had a great day. But I realised that football fitness is so different to any other sort of fitness. It was a great experience, but so hard on that Old Trafford pitch. You don't realise how big it is until you step on it! I was playing on the left and I had Harry Redknapp telling me to make sure I support the attack when we go forward, but when the ball comes back he needs me tracking back to cover for Gary Cahill. I did one run back and I was blowing!

You played the whole of the first half of that Soccer Aid game against the Rest of the World XI, with an Arsenal legend with you in midfield...
Yes what an experience! I will never ever forget that day. I was actually with Jack Wilshere for most of the day and he's such a top lad. I sat next to him on the coach, we had a great chat, and it turns out he lives near me as well. It was great to be with him, and then of course to be on the pitch alongside him was incredible. But I got on with everyone there, they were all really good fun. David Seaman too – what a legend! We were in a training camp for three days before the game and it was brilliant. He must have been such a good person to have round the dressing room back in the day because he's a leader, he was organising the night out, getting the lads together, he was quality!

MIDFIELDER

KAI HAVERTZ

29

Born: Aachen, Germany, June 11, 1999

Nationality: German

Joined: from Chelsea on June 28, 2023

Previous clubs: Bayer Leverkusen, Chelsea

Debut: v Manchester City (n), Community Shield, August 6, 2023 (drew 1-1, won on penalties)

Skilful Germany international Kai became our first signing of the summer transfer window in 2023 when he signed in a big money move from Chelsea. Versatile, strong on either foot and attack-minded, Kai spent three seasons with the west London club, impressing with his pressing, creativity, eye for goal and aerial strength. He netted at a rate of nearly one every three games, including winning strikes in both the 2021 Champions League final against Manchester City, and 2022 FIFA Club World Cup final against Palmeiras. A vital part of the Germany national team, he made his senior debut for his country in 2018 at the age of 19. Before moving to the Premier League he had played all his football for Bayer Leverkusen, being named in the Bundesliga Team of the Season in 2018/19. He was part of the Germany squad at the 2022 World Cup, scoring twice in the group stage win over Costa Rica.

MIDFIELDER

DECLAN RICE

41

Born: Kingston-upon-Thames, January 14, 1999

Nationality: English

Joined: from West Ham United on July 15, 2023

Previous club: West Ham United

Debut: v Manchester City (n), Community Shield, August 6, 2023 (drew 1-1, won on penalties)

First goal: v Manchester United (h), Premier League, September 3, 2023 (won 3-1)

England international midfielder Declan joined in a high-profile move in the summer, having captained previous club West Ham to Europa Conference success last season. A tenacious, clever, disciplined and dominant central midfielder, he made nearly 250 appearances for the Hammers, barely missing a game in the past five seasons. His first senior goal actually came against us, in January 2019, while still a teenager. He was named West Ham Young Player of the Year three times, and Player of the Year in each of the past two campaigns. With Irish grandparents, Declan was eligible to play for the Republic of Ireland, and won three caps for them before switching to England. He played at Euro 2020, helping Gareth Southgate's side to reach the final, and played in all five matches at the 2022 World Cup in Qatar.

THE
ENORMOUS
ARSENAL QUIZ

30 questions all about the greatest club in the world! Good luck!

1. From which club did we sign Thomas Partey?

2. What nationality is Leandro Trossard?

3. Which visiting team has conceded the most overall goals at Emirates Stadium?

4. What is our record win in Premier League history?

5. Which player has the most all-time Premier League assists for us?

6. At which stadium did Mikel Arteta start his managerial career with us?

7. How old was Gabriel Martinelli when he made his Arsenal debut?

8. Who is the youngest player to appear for the Arsenal first team?

9. Which team did we beat in the 2006 Champions League semi-final?

10. How many times have we won the FA Cup?

11. Who was the first Spaniard to play for Arsenal?

12. Against which team did William Saliba make his Arsenal debut?

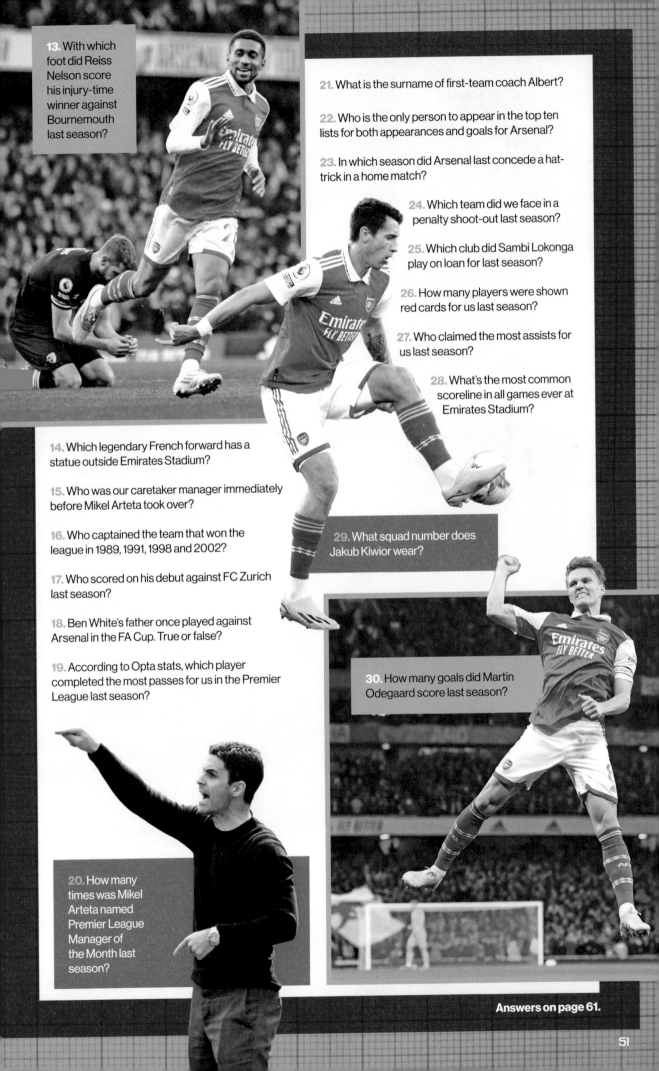

13. With which foot did Reiss Nelson score his injury-time winner against Bournemouth last season?

21. What is the surname of first-team coach Albert?

22. Who is the only person to appear in the top ten lists for both appearances and goals for Arsenal?

23. In which season did Arsenal last concede a hat-trick in a home match?

24. Which team did we face in a penalty shoot-out last season?

25. Which club did Sambi Lokonga play on loan for last season?

26. How many players were shown red cards for us last season?

27. Who claimed the most assists for us last season?

28. What's the most common scoreline in all games ever at Emirates Stadium?

14. Which legendary French forward has a statue outside Emirates Stadium?

15. Who was our caretaker manager immediately before Mikel Arteta took over?

16. Who captained the team that won the league in 1989, 1991, 1998 and 2002?

17. Who scored on his debut against FC Zurich last season?

18. Ben White's father once played against Arsenal in the FA Cup. True or false?

19. According to Opta stats, which player completed the most passes for us in the Premier League last season?

29. What squad number does Jakub Kiwior wear?

30. How many goals did Martin Odegaard score last season?

20. How many times was Mikel Arteta named Premier League Manager of the Month last season?

Answers on page 61.

DEFENDER

JURRIEN TIMBER

12

Born: Utrecht, Netherlands, June 17, 2001

Nationality: Dutch

Joined: from Ajax on July 14, 2023

Previous club: Ajax

Debut: v Manchester City (n), Community Shield, August 6, 2023 (drew 1-1, won on penalties)

A versatile and technically sound defender, Jurrien joined from Ajax in the summer, after a wonderful season for both club and country. Usually used in central defence for Ajax, he is also comfortable in either full back position, using his speed, reading of the game and superb passing range to great effect when bringing the ball forward. He made his first team debut for Ajax at the age of 18, and won back-to-back league titles for the Amsterdam club, and also became a full international for the Netherlands while still a teenager. He played four times for his country at the 2022 World Cup in Qatar, having been part of the team that won the Under-17 European Championships in 2018, alongside his twin brother Quinten. A youth international from the Under-15 age group onwards, his brother Dylan is also a professional footballer in the Netherlands, and represents Curacao at international level (their father's nationality).

GOALKEEPER

DAVID RAYA

22

Born: Barcelona, Spain,
September 15, 1995

Nationality: Spanish

Joined (on loan): from Brentford
on August 15, 2023

Previous clubs:
Blackburn Rovers, Southport
(loan), Brentford

Spain international goalkeeper David joined us on a season-long loan from fellow Premier League side Brentford right at the start of the season. He had been the regular No. 1 for the Bees for four seasons, winning the Championship Golden Glove award in his debut year, for most clean sheets in the division. He then barely missed a game as he helped Brentford earn promotion to the Premier League in 2021, winning the Play-Off final at Wembley. Known as a sweeper-keeper who can instigate attacks from in or around his own penalty area, the Spaniard was ever-present last season, and was nominated for the Premier League Player of the Month award in January for his superb form. Before starring at Brentford David spent five seasons at Blackburn Rovers, helping them to promotion from League One in 2018. An accomplished shot-stopper and superb with the ball at his feet, he was part of Spain's World Cup squad for the tournament in Qatar in 2022.

53

COMPETITION
WIN A SIGNED SHIRT!

Just answer the following question to be in with a chance of winning.

Who won the Arsenal.com Player of the Year award last season?

A Martin Odegaard
B Bukayo Saka
C Gabriel Martinelli

Entry is by email only. Only one entry per contestant. Please enter **AFC SHIRT** followed by either **A, B or C** in the subject line of an email. In the body of the email, please include your full name, address, postcode, email address and phone number and send to:
frontdesk@grangecommunications.co.uk
by Sunday 31st March 2024.

WORDSEARCH

Can you find these past and present Arsenal Women?

E	Q	I	Q	C	Q	R	E	S	K	V	N
T	L	T	T	S	F	I	M	O	G	R	O
A	U	T	C	L	T	Y	H	Z	O	M	S
K	E	O	T	F	A	Y	B	V	U	I	M
L	T	L	N	I	E	W	I	Z	C	E	A
T	Z	K	K	K	L	C	N	E	W	D	I
M	L	P	N	R	M	A	B	G	O	E	L
G	E	A	Z	N	X	A	D	W	L	M	L
S	Y	A	N	H	C	E	N	R	D	A	I
C	M	R	D	C	M	A	A	N	U	M	W
H	T	I	M	S	Q	Q	A	V	L	L	V
A	D	E	E	H	M	S	L	G	A	J	X

LITTLE	MEAD	WALTI
LUDLOW	MIEDEMA	WILLIAMSON
MCCABE	SCOTT	YANKEY
MAANUM	SMITH	

Answers on page 61.

EMIRATES MAKEOVER!

Emirates Stadium underwent a drastic change of appearance last season, as the eight huge murals that adorn the side of the venue were all replaced with brand new artwork. The eight pieces were devised and designed in consultation with our global supporter base, and were the result of months of planning and production across the club.

The new installations pay tribute to the club's illustrious and proud history, while also looking ahead and celebrating our magnificent worldwide Gunners community. Here's a bit more info about each one…

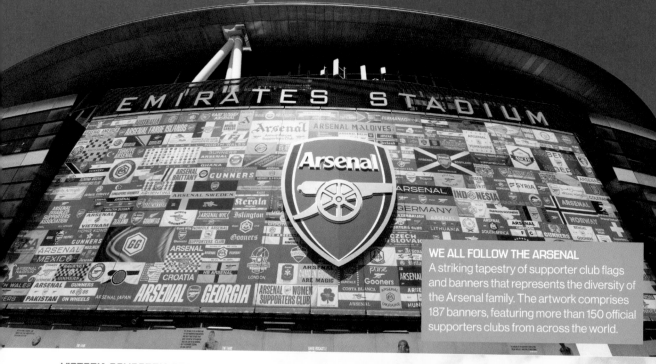

WE ALL FOLLOW THE ARSENAL
A striking tapestry of supporter club flags and banners that represents the diversity of the Arsenal family. The artwork comprises 187 banners, featuring more than 150 official supporters clubs from across the world.

VICTORIA CONCORDIA CRESCIT
This piece tells the story of our iconic players who embody the spirit of the Gunners. Legends are shown alongside our famous cannons with flags emblazoned with the club's motto: Victoria Concordia Crescit – Victory Through Harmony. The players featured are: George Male, Martin Keown, Emma Byrne, Jayne Ludlow, Ian Wright, Eddie Hapgood, Alex Scott, Marieanne Spacey, Frank McLintock, David Seaman, Tony Adams and David Rocastle.

FUTURE BRILLIANCE
This artwork is inspired by Arsène Wenger's quote: "Here you have the opportunity to get out the greatness that is in each of you," and it celebrates our rich and long-standing devotion to producing young talent. Players included: Charlie George, Jack Wilshere, David O'Leary, Kelly Smith, Rachel Yankey, Paul Davis, Paul Merson, Lianne Sanderson, Pat Rice, Liam Brady and Tony Adams.

REMEMBER WHO YOU ARE

A stunning representation of the famous East Stand façade at our former home, Highbury. Some of the greatest players and managers from our history are included on the artwork, with many references to significant club moments also to be found within the design. The personalities featured are: Kirsty Pealling, John Radford, Alan Smith, Sian Williams, Faye White, David Jack, Kenny Sansom, Cliff Bastin, Ian Wright, Thierry Henry, Ted Drake, David Danskin, Ken Friar, Arsène Wenger, Bob Wilson, David Seaman, Pat Rice, Alex James, Jack Kelsey, George Armstrong, Michael Thomas, David Rocastle, Kevin Campbell, Paul Davis, Reg Lewis, Joe Mercer, Herbert Chapman, George Graham, Bertie Mee, Lee Dixon, Tony Adams, Steve Bould and Nigel Winterburn.

COME TO SEE THE ARSENAL

A bold, type-based design that celebrates our community roots in north London, that has been home to the Gunners since we moved to Highbury in 1913.

FOUND A PLACE WHERE WE BELONG

This is the ultimate illustrated crowd scene, representing the importance of the Arsenal family. The artwork brings together more than 700 supporters who have contributed to the club's success, given so much to the community and followed us through thick and thin.

INVINCIBLE

Celebrating two of the most famous achievements in the club's history – the women's team becoming the first English side to win the Champions League in 2006/07, and Arsène Wenger's Invincibles of 2003/04. Men's team included: Dennis Bergkamp, Patrick Vieira, Ray Parlour, Thierry Henry, Arsène Wenger, Robert Pires, Freddie Ljungberg, Sol Campbell, Gilberto, Kolo Toure, Lauren, Edu, Jens Lehmann and Ashley Cole.
Women's team included: Anita Asante, Julie Fleeting, Lianne Sanderson, Alex Scott, Jayne Ludlow, Katie Chapman, Rachel Yankey, Mary Phillip, Ciara Grant, Kelly Smith, Vic Akers, Karen Carney, Emma Byrne and Faye White.

EIGHTEEN EIGHTY-SIX

Another type-based artwork, that symbolises our founding year in Woolwich, and the constant pursuit of progress ever since.

ARSENAL WOMEN

Think you know about the women's team? Try these multiple choice questions...

1. Who is pictured here?
A) Lia Walti
B) Lotte Wubben-Moy
C) Victoria Pelova

2. Who did we beat in last season's Continental Cup final?
A) Manchester United
B) Manchester City
C) Chelsea

3. Who was our top goalscorer last season?
A) Stina Blackstenius
B) Frida Maanum
C) Caitlin Foord

4. What nationality is Kathrine Kuhl?
A) Swedish
B) Dutch
C) Danish

5. In which year did Arsenal win the European Cup?
A) 2004
B) 2007
C) 2010

6. How many times have Arsenal Women won the FA Cup?
A) 14
B) 16
C) 18

7. What was the attendance when we faced Wolfsburg at home last season?
A) 56,766
B) 58,299
C) 60,063

8. What squad number does Katie McCabe wear?
A) 3
B) 11
C) 15

9. As well as Emirates Stadium, where else do Arsenal Women play home games?
A) Meadow Park
B) Vicarage Road
C) The Hive Stadium

10. Who is the leading all-time scorer in the current squad?
A) Vivianne Miedema
B) Beth Mead
C) Kim Little

Answers on page 61.

LET'S CELEBRATE!

Can you guess the player from the celebration?

Answers on page 61.

JUNIOR GUNNERS

Become a Junior Gunner!

Junior Gunners is the youth membership scheme for Arsenal supporters aged 0-16 years. Our JG members receive access to a range of exclusive benefits, including:

• **Seasonal membership pack***
• **Access to Arsenal experiences including opportunities to meet players**
• **The chance to be a mascot or part of the Arsenal Ball Squad**
• **And much more!**

To find out more, and to join, head to arsenal.com/membership/junior

*Full Membership Only

QUIZ ANSWERS

Goals, goals, goals (page 20)
1. C) Jakub Kiwior
2. C) Kieran Trippier
3. A) 8
4. A) North Bank
5. C) Bournemouth
6. A) Martin Odegaard
7. B) 3-2
8. B) 96:57
9. C) Gabriel Jesus
10. B) 4
11. C) Eddie Nketiah
12. B) Right foot

Gabby, Gabi or Gabi?! (page 21)
1. Gabriel Martinelli
2. Gabriel Jesus
3. Gabriel Magalhaes
4. Gabriel Jesus
5. Gabriel Magalhaes
6. Gabriel Martinelli
7. Gabriel Martinelli
8. Gabriel Jesus
9. Gabriel Magalhaes
10. Gabriel Jesus

Who Am I? (page 36)
1. Thierry Henry
2. Tony Adams
3. Patrick Vieira
4. Bukayo Saka
5. Santi Cazorla
6. Gabriel Martinelli
7. William Saliba
8. Martin Odegaard
9. David Seaman
10. Gabriel Jesus
11. Ben White
12. Robert Pires
13. Ian Wright
14. Leandro Trossard

Spot the Difference (page 37)

The Enormous Arsenal Quiz (page 50)
1. Atletico Madrid
2. Belgian
3. Tottenham Hotspur
4. 7-0
5. Dennis Bergkamp
6. Vitality Stadium
7. 18
8. Ethan Nwaneri
9. Villarreal
10. 14
11. Cesc Fabregas
12. Crystal Palace
13. Left
14. Thierry Henry
15. Freddie Ljungberg
16. Tony Adams
17. Marquinhos
18. False
19. Gabriel
20. Four
21. Stuivenberg
22. John Radford
23. 1993/94
24. Sporting
25. Crystal Palace
26. None
27. Bukayo Saka
28. 2-0
29. 15
30. 15

Wordsearch (page 55)

Q	Q	L	Q	C	Q	R	E	S	K	V
T	T	T	S	F	I	M	O	G	R	Q
A	U	E	E	T	Y	H	Z	O	M	M
K	E	Q	F	E	B	V	U	E
L	L	N	E	E	V	I	Z	C	E
V	Z	K	K	E	C	N	E	V
E	L	P	N	R	M	A	G	E
G	A	Z	N	X	D	W	E
S	Y	N	H	E	N	R	E
C	M	R	E	E	E	E	E
H	T	L	E	Q	Q	A	V	L	V
A	D	E	E	H	M	S	L	G	A	J	X

Arsenal Women (page 58)
1. Lia Walti
2. Chelsea
3. Stina Blackstenius
4. Danish
5. 2007
6. 14
7. 60,063
8. 15
9. Meadow Park
10. Kim Little

Let's Celebrate (page 59)
1. Bukayo Saka
2. Gabriel Jesus
3. Gabriel Martinelli
4. Martin Odegaard
5. Eddie Nketiah
6. William Saliba

WHERE'S GUNNERSAURUS?